PRO SPORTS
BIOGRAPHIES

AARON RODGERS

by Allan Morey

AMICUS | AMICUS INK

Amicus High Interest and Amicus Ink are published by Amicus
P.O. Box 1329, Mankato, MN 56002
www.amicuspublishing.us

Library of Congress Cataloging-in-Publications Data
Names: Morey, Allan, author.
Title: Aaron Rodgers / by Allan Morey.
Description: Mankato, Minnesota : Amicus/Amicus Ink, [2020] | Series: Pro sport biographies | Includes index. | Audience: Grades: K–3.
Identifiers: LCCN 2018039463 (print) | LCCN 2019002365 (ebook) | ISBN 9781681517452 (pdf) | ISBN 9781681516639 (library binding) | ISBN 9781681524498 (pbk.)
Subjects: LCSH: Rodgers, Aaron, 1983—Juvenile literature. | Football players—United States—Biography—Juvenile literature. | Quarterbacks (Football)—United States—Biography—Juvenile literature.
Classification: LCC GV939.R6235 (ebook) | LCC GV939.R6235 M66 2020 (print) | DDC 796.332092 [B]--dc23
LC record available at https://lccn.loc.gov/2018039463

Photo Credits: Alamy/Margaret Bowles, CSM cover; Alamy/Paul Kitagaki Jr., ZUMA Wire 2; Alamy/John Pyle, Cal Sport Media 4–5; Jeff Jordan, Butte College 6–7; Newscom/Dilip Vishwanat, Sporting News, Icon SMI 8; Getty/Chris Trotman, Stringer 10–11; AP/Mike Roemer 12; AP/David Stluka, STLUD 15; AP/Mark Humphrey 16–17; Getty/Jamie Squire 18–19; Getty/Dylan Buell 20; WikiCommons/Keith Allison 22

Editors: Wendy Dieker and Alissa Thielges
Designer: Aubrey Harper
Photo Researcher: Holly Young

Printed in the United States of America

HC 10 9 8 7 6 5 4 3 2 1
PB 10 9 8 7 6 5 4 3 2 1

TABLE OF CONTENTS

4

TOUCHDOWN!

Aaron Rodgers steps back to pass. He tosses the football. It is caught in the **end zone**. Touchdown! Rodgers is a **quarterback**. He plays for the Green Bay Packers.

YOUNG STAR

Rodgers grew up in Chico, California. He played quarterback in high school. He then went to Butte College in Oroville, California. He led the school's football team to a 10-1 record.

Aaron could throw a football through a hanging tire when he was 5 years old.

BIGGER AND BETTER

Butte College was a small school. Rodgers wanted to show off his skills at a bigger college. He went to the University of California at Berkeley. He became a top quarterback in college.

TURNING PRO

In 2005, Rodgers turned pro. He was **drafted** by the Green Bay Packers. They picked him in the first round of the draft. They hoped Rodgers would be a future star for their team.

A BACKUP

Rodgers began as a **backup**. The Packers already had a star quarterback. His name was Brett Favre. Rodgers learned how to play in the NFL by watching him.

A ROUGH START

In 2008, it was Rodgers's time to
start. He had a rough season.
The Packers only won 6 games.
Rodgers played better the next
year. The Packers won 11 games.

SUPER BOWL

In 2011, Rodgers led the Packers to the Super Bowl. They faced the Pittsburgh Steelers. Rodgers threw three touchdowns in the game. He helped the Packers win!

Rodgers was named the MVP of the 2011 Super Bowl.

RUNNING THE BALL

Rodgers is a great passer. He can zip the ball down the field. But he is also a good rusher. He can run with the ball down the field, too.

Rodgers has more than 20 rushing touchdowns.

THE FUTURE

Rodgers continues to throw touchdowns. He led the Packers to the **playoffs** eight years in a row. He hopes to lead the Packers back to the Super Bowl.

JUST THE FACTS

Born: December 2, 1983

Hometown: Chico, California

Colleges: Butte College; University of California, Berkley

Joined the pros: 2005

Draft: Round 1, Pick 24

Position: Quarterback

Stats: www.nfl.com/player/ aaronrodgers/2506363/profile

Accomplishments:

- Pro Bowl Appearances: 2018, 2016, 2015, 2014, 2012, 2011, 2009

- Led the NFL in Most touchdowns: 2016 (40)

- Associated Press Player of the Year: 2014, 2011

- Super Bowl Victories: 2011

WORDS TO KNOW

backup – a support player who enters the game if another player can't play

drafted – to be picked to play for a team

end zone – the area at either end of a football field

playoffs – series of games to determine which teams will play in the championship game

quarterback – player who runs a team's offense; he throws the ball to receivers and hands the ball off to runners

start – to be one of the players who is on the field at the beginning of the game

LEARN MORE

Books
Maurer, Tracy Nelson. *Aaron Rodgers*. North Mankato, Minn.: Capstone Press, 2016.

Morey, Allan. *The Green Bay Packers Story*. Minneapolis: Bellwether Media, Inc., 2017.

Osborne, M.K. *Superstars of the Green Bay Packers*. Mankato, Minn: Amicus, 2019.

Websites
ESPN | Aaron Rodgers
www.espn.com/nfl/player/_/id/8439/aaron-rodgers

Green Bay Packers
https://www.packers.com

INDEX